PURPOSELY POSITIONED

Tisha Jones

Diligence Publishing Company
Bloomfield, New Jersey

The Scripture in this book is from the King James Version and the New International Version.

PURPOSELY POSITIONED

To contact Tisha Jones to preach or speak at your church, organization, seminar or conference email:

purposelypositioned50@gmail.com

PURPOSELY POSITIONED

ISBN: 978-1-7331353-5-1

Printed in the United States

TABLE OF CONTENTS

DEDICATION

I am dedicating this book to my husband Sylvester Jones and my son Caleb Isaiah Woodley. I love you, and I thank God for you both because I know He has Purposely Positioned you in my life.

FOREWORD

The Body of Christ, also known as the Church, is in a fight like never before against spiritual wickedness that lurks and thrives in darkness and dark places. I describe these places as unrevealed and unexposed realities.

In this book, Pastor Tisha Jones turns the light on to reveal and expose the realities of relationships by using her own experiences.

This transparency, I am certain, will be relatable as well as a powerful tool for deliverance! Every reader will, through these pages, realize that we serve a God of purpose who takes our ups and downs to position us for our great future that awaits us!

Be blessed as you read this amazing book and realize that like Pastor Tisha Jones, you too are "PURPOSELY POSITIONED!"

Bishop T. Raynard Randall
TH.B., TH.M., M.R.E.

ACKNOWLEDGEMENTS

I would like to thank everyone who played a major role in my walk with Christ. I cannot write everyone's name, but I thank you and love you all. There are some people I must acknowledge. To my wonderful, loving, and patient husband, Sly, who has been Purposely Positioned in my life.

To my son Caleb, I love you with all my heart; you are my prince. To my parents, you have been the best examples for me to live by. I love you. To my siblings: Kim, Robert, Keisha, and Chasidy, I love you dearly. To my nieces and nephew: Shae and Dionna you are beautiful women. God has so much for you. Brandon, it's not where you are, it's where you're going. Trust God. Keeley, you are strong and courageous, and I can't wait to see the greatness that comes out of you. Know that God has His hand on you. I'm so proud of you!

Pastor Ieisha, thank you for seeing greatness in me, for not letting me give up, and for staying on this journey with me.

To my first Pastor, Overseer Broughton and Co-Pastor Marilyn Broughton, thank you for always praying for me and teaching me how to serve in love.

Bishop Loretta Smith-Johnson, thank you for teaching me how to use my gifts. It was an honor to serve you.

To my Shepherd, Bishop T. Raynard Randall, thank you for trusting the voice of God concerning the ministry in me, and thank you for being a wonderful man of God.

To my Lord and Savior, the one and the only true living God, where would I be without you!

CHAPTER 1

My Tragedy Turned Into My Miracle

I was married at 19 to the first man who said, "I love you." I said, "I will show all those who told me no one would want to marry me because I was overweight. They will see that someone does love me, and he wants to be with me."

How do you love yourself or someone else when you don't know what that looks or feels like? I knew I wanted to be loved, so I said yes. We got married at the courthouse. He had a hangover from the night before. My twin sister and our best friend stood by my side as I said, "I do!"

After the wedding, we stayed in a hotel for two days. He was hung over for the first night. I thought, I could be with my sister right now and return when he sobers up. My twin and I did everything together. She was my ride or die. We told each other everything. We did everything together. We even got into trouble together. Well honestly, I got into trouble because of her, but I didn't care. I always wanted to protect her. I was the quiet one, and she was the social butterfly. She always wanted to go out to parties and hang out in the mall or with her boyfriend.

The rule of our house was we had to go out together or not at all, so when she wanted to go to a party or be with her boyfriend, I would have to go too. We would leave out together, go our separate ways, and meet up again later at the corner of our house. I would go to a friend's house and wait until she called me, and later I would meet her on the corner, and we would walk into the house together with no one being the wiser. That was our routine, and it worked for us. She would tell me all about her evening, and I would live my life through her adventures. I always thought she was so beautiful, and because I never thought I was pretty, I believe this is why I was not so social.

We couldn't do a lot growing up, but what we could do, we did with a bang. We spent every summer working at my grandmother's store, which was fun because we had a little more freedom. My sister was always the popular one with the boys, and one boy in particular caught her attention. Keith was a new boy around my grandmother's store, and he had money to spend. He was older than her, but that didn't stop him from pursuing my sister. I knew he was trouble when I first saw him. He showered her with gifts, money, and attention. She fell fast and hard, and he moved her away from me to another state. This state would change her forever and me too.

I was living with my husband's parents and learning how to be a wife at 19. I believed my husband really loved me, and I loved him because he loved me. I didn't know the first thing about being a wife. All I knew was I had to cook, clean, have sex, and make my husband happy. And that's what I did. He worked, and I stayed home and took care of the house. What else was I supposed to do? I didn't know any better.

Marriage was good for the first few years. I was happy, and my husband treated me good, but I felt something was missing. I didn't spend much time with my family. My sister was in another state, so I only had him and his family. I was okay with that because I felt loved. After a couple of years of living with his parents, we finally got our own apartment. I was so happy. He furnished our whole apartment. Everything was brand new and beautiful.

I went to the mailbox every afternoon like clockwork. We had been in our own place for one year, and one day as I went to get the mail, I noticed a piece of paper taped to our door with the words "EVICTION NOTICE" on it. I grabbed the mail, took the paper off the door, and went into the house. I began to read the notice and it said, "You have 10 days to evacuate the premises, or you will be locked out."

I couldn't believe what I was reading. I immediately called my husband and asked him what was going on and where would we go if we got evicted. I was so amazed at how calm he was. He told me not to worry about it. He would take care of it. I calmed down and believed he would take care of it. After all, he paid all the bills. Eight days later, there was a knock on the door and a man said, "We are from Furniture Rentals,"

I said, "Hello. How can I help you?"

He said, "I'm here to pick up your furniture, so please step aside."

I stood in shock in the hallway of our apartment as these two huge men took all our furniture out of our apartment and loaded it up on their truck. I couldn't call my husband because he was traveling home by train, and there were no cell phones then. Thirty minutes later, he walked in the door to find me balled up in the corner on the living room floor where my beautiful living room set used to be. I was crying hysterically. He looked around and realized why I was crying, and he said, "It's going to be alright. I'll get more furniture."

I jumped up and screamed and said, "What are you talking about?"

He said, "I rented the furniture, and I missed a couple of payments."

"A couple of payments!" I said.

Then he said, "So they had to come and get the furniture. Since we have to move, I stopped paying them."

I fell to the floor and cried for an hour because I just didn't understand what was going on. After all, he told me he would take care of everything. I was so young and naive. I had no idea you could rent furniture and make weekly payments, and I definitely never experienced being put out of an apartment. Why would I? This never happened to me before. I went straight from my parents' house to his parents' house.

That day I grew up and realized that the honeymoon was over for real. Ten years and ten apartments later, I was fed up with him and my life. I needed a change right away. I bought a one-way ticket to go and stay with my sister in Virginia. I waited until he left for work. Then I packed my clothes in a suitcase and headed for the train station. Ten hours later, I arrived at my sister's house. I was so happy to be with my sister again.

For the next week, I did not call him or want to talk to him. I felt free. The next week, I started looking for a job so I could find myself an apartment. I went on a job interview, and I was hired. That night we went out, and we celebrated. After dinner, my sister's phone kept ringing, and I said, "Who keeps calling you, and why won't you answer the phone?"

She said, "It's not for me. It's for you."

I said, "For me? Who is it?"

She sucked her teeth and said, "Girl please! He's been calling you since you arrived, but I kept telling him you were not available. But now I'm sick of him calling. Please answer the phone so he can stop ringing my phone to death."

I was happy and sad at the same time because I was starting to miss him. I picked up the phone, and he said, "Please come back. I love you, and I miss you."

I said, "No. I'm tired of arguing with you, and I'm tired of moving."

He called every day for the next three weeks, and then the calls stopped. It was a Saturday morning. I got up, did my usual routine, and went to work. All of a sudden, I hear my name being called on the intercom throughout the store to come to the front of the store for a visitor. I started walking to the front of the store expecting to see my sister, but to my surprise, it was my husband. I couldn't believe my eyes. I said to myself, *"I can't believe this man came all the way here without calling me first."* I walked up to him and asked him, "What are you doing here?"

He said, "Surprise!"

I said again, "What are you doing here?"

He said, "I left my job to move here with you."

I didn't know if I should smack him or run. I started hitting him on the arm and said, "Follow me," because I didn't want to make a scene. As soon as we got outside, I started cussing him out like a sailor. I was furious at him, but I was glad

17

to see him too. I called my sister and told her what just happened.

The first thing she said was, "Where is he going to stay?"

I knew then we had to get our own apartment sooner than later. She was not happy about him staying with us, but she let him stay. He got a job, and one month later, we moved into our own apartment. Three years and three apartments later, we were still doing the same thing.

I always wanted kids but was never able to conceive. I always thought it was because I never had a regular menstrual cycle and somehow that affected my hormones. One day, I decided to go to the OB/GYN and see why I was never able to have kids. The doctor took all kinds of tests and blood work and told me she would call me when the results came back. Three days later, I was cooking, and the phone rang. It was my doctor, and she asked me if I was sitting down. I said, "No, I'm actually cooking right now."

She said, "Please sit down." So I did, and she began to tell me that my results came back, and she said, "You have stage three cancer in the uterus."

My mouth dropped open and I said, "What did you say?"

She repeated it again and said, "I am scheduling you for surgery immediately to perform a full hysterectomy."

The first scripture that came to my mind was, *"When Jesus heard that, He said, "This sickness is not unto death, but for the glory of God, that the Son of God may be glorified through it."* (John 11:4)

I began to cry. My husband ran out of the bedroom and just began to hold me. He asked me what was wrong.

The doctor was still on the line. She said, "I will call you in the morning so we can discuss all of your options."

I told my husband what the doctor said. He immediately started to cry and then he said, "We will be okay."

I stopped crying and called my mother and told her the news. She just prayed and said, "God is in control, and I am not moved." We talked for a long time, and at the end of our conversation, my mom asked me if I wanted to receive Jesus Christ as my Savior. I said yes. I repeated the sinner's prayer and received Jesus as my Lord and Savior in February 2001.

The next day, my doctor called and set a date for my surgery. My full hysterectomy was scheduled for February 14, 2001. My mom and my sister drove from New Jersey to be with me during my surgery. I'll never forget laying on the hospital bed getting prepped for surgery. As I was being rolled down the hospital hallway towards the operating room, I looked back at my family and said to God, "If you allow me to see my family again, you will never have to worry about me ever again." I woke up praising God.

After my surgery, I decided to move back to New Jersey to be closer to my family. My husband wasn't in agreement, so he stayed in Virginia. I stayed with my mom, got a job, and joined a church. Three months later, I moved into my own apartment, and one month later, my husband was back in New Jersey. He got a job, and we both started attending church. My husband never went to church as a child, so this was new to him, but because he loved me, he wanted us to go to church as a family.

Everything seemed to be better with us because we were going to church, and I was falling in love with myself because of my growing relationship with God. We started serving in ministry, and life was good. After a year in ministry, my husband was serving as an Armor Bearer and was ordained as a Deacon, and I was also serving as an Armor Bearer and a Minister in Training. I loved serving in ministry and serving my pastors. It made me feel good when I served.

I still had a longing feeling for a child that would not go away, but I knew that it would not be possible after having stage three cancer and a full hysterectomy. So I tried not to think about it, but I couldn't help feeling that it was a punishment because of my lifestyle before I received Christ. I became angry with God because I didn't understand why I was the one who couldn't have kids. I never smoked, did drugs, hung out in the streets, or hurt anyone. I wasn't a bad person. I knew I would have been a great mom.

I continued to serve in ministry and stayed faithful to my church and my pastors. I had to ask God to forgive me for being angry with Him because I know that God does not cause bad things to happen to us. He loves us and wants the best for us. On Sunday, October 23, 2005, our church had a guest speaker named Prophetess Priscilla. I was serving on the Pastoral Care Committee in the kitchen. All of a sudden, I heard the Prophetess say, "Where is your wife? Go get your wife."

As soon as I looked up, Mother Mamie came through the kitchen door, pulled me by the arm and said, "The Prophetess is calling you."

As soon as I walked through the sanctuary doors, the Prophetess asked me, "Is this your husband?"

I said, "Yes."

She said, "Come and stand by him." She looked at me and said, "God is going to bless you with a baby."

I looked at my husband and then at my pastor and thought to myself, *"If God puts a baby in this womb, I'm going straight to someone's talk show and make some money because it would definitely be a miracle."*

She told us to lift our hands, and she prayed for us. On October 28th, five days later, my pastor called me and said the Prophetess had called and left her phone number for me to call her. I wrote the number down and called the Prophetess. As soon as I said hello, she said, "I keep having this same dream that a baby is face down in a toilet, and when I reach down to grab the baby, it's your face that I see." Then she said, "I need you to pray for this baby."

I hung up the phone and began to pray. I didn't know where this baby was, but I just prayed. Almost two weeks later, On November 8, 2005, I was still praying, but on this particular day, I felt sad and my spirit was weeping as if I was mourning the death of someone.

I received a phone call while I was at lunch. I answered the phone and said, "Hello," but there was no answer, so I said, "Hello" again.

A voice on the other end said, "She died on the operating table giving birth."

I recognized my brother's voice, and I said, "Who died?"

He said, "My girlfriend died giving birth, and I'm calling you to ask you if you would take the baby and raise him as your son."

I was shocked because I didn't know his girlfriend was pregnant. I didn't even hesitate. I said, "Yes, of course."

I left the job and went straight to the hospital. I arrived at the hospital, and the mother of my brother's girlfriend met me on the maternity ward.

As soon as I said, "I'm so sorry for your loss," she said, "My daughter only met you one time, but she told me if anything happened to her, she wanted you to take care of her child."

At that moment I understood the meaning of the prophet's dream and began to give God praise.

Then her mom took me to see the baby. He was a beautiful baby boy. The nurse took me inside the nursery and said, "The baby needs to feel the warmth of his mother."

I began to cry and praise God for His faithfulness to me. I held my son in my arms and began to sing to him. I asked God, "What is his name?"

God said, "Give him a name from my Word."

I said, "His name will be Caleb, because he will pull down the strongholds and conquer the land." Caleb was born on November 7, 2005. The next day, my husband and I went to the hospital with a brand-new car seat to pick up our son. We smiled and laughed all the way down the parking lot to the hospital at the goodness of the Lord.

I took a leave of absence from my job to take care of Caleb and stayed home to raise him. Three years and three apartments later, my husband stopped going to church, and by the time Caleb was almost turning four, our marriage was on its last leg. We tried counseling, but my husband refused to go after the second session. When I returned home from the session, he had moved out of the bedroom into the living room. After that, he barely spoke to me anymore. The following Sunday, Caleb and I came home from church, we walked into the apartment, and my husband looked so mad. He just started arguing as soon as I closed the door. I sat Caleb on the couch and turned to my husband and said, "What's wrong now?"

As soon as I looked in his eyes, I knew it wasn't going to be a good night. He frowned up his face like I've never seen before. He balled up his fist and I said, "If you hit me, you will go to jail today."

He looked at me and put his fist down and said repeatedly, "I can't wait for you to leave my apartment. I'll be glad when you get out of my apartment. Why don't you leave because I do not want you here anymore? Get out before I" As soon as he said, "Before I," I grabbed Caleb, ran to the bedroom, locked the door, and called my pastor to pray for us. He came banging on the bedroom door, screaming and yelling for me to get out of his apartment before he throws me out. He was banging and kicking the door.

I stood by the door to make sure it was locked. I repeatedly said, "Leave me alone."

After a few minutes of listening to his heavy breathing and then silence, I started praying and he walked away from the door. I could hear the TV, so I turned away from the door and sat on the bed. I began to pray, and I said to God, "God, you have to get me out of this situation before he hurts me and causes me to go to jail."

That was the worst night I had in our twenty-year marriage. It was like my life had turned into a nightmare. I didn't sleep all night watching the door, scared he would kick it down and come in and hurt me. The next day, I was leaving the apartment to pick Caleb up from the daycare, and my landlord stopped me and asked me if I was looking for an apartment. I hesitated because I had just asked God the night before to get me out of my bad situation, and the next day I'm offered an apartment. I looked at my landlord and said, "Yes, I am, but I do not have any security money."

He said, "Don't worry. I will take the security money from the apartment you're in now and put it on the apartment I'm going to rent to you, and your husband will have to pay the security for his apartment." I was so amazed at the hand of God because I never told anyone about what happened, and I knew this was God. He told me he had a one-bedroom apartment right around the corner on the next block, I could move in by the weekend, and my first month's rent was free.

I wanted to kiss that white man like he was Santa Claus, but I knew he was an angel sent by God, so I held my composure. When he left, I got in my car and worshipped God until I got tired and had no voice. On Saturday morning, my husband left for work, and I called a friend to help me move. I didn't take anything but our clothes. I didn't want anything but my freedom, especially when I knew God had freed me. God made a way for me to move out, take the security money and transfer it to my new apartment, get one month free, and move without any trouble. I signed my lease, and in April of 2010, I moved into my new apartment.

When my husband returned home from work, he noticed there was no one there. He called my cell phone and asked me why I wasn't home yet.

I said, "That is not my home anymore."

27

He got quiet and said, "Please come back. I'm sorry."

I replied, "Yes you are!" Then I said, "No, you left the marriage one year ago when you stopped talking to me, stopped eating my food, moved out of the bedroom, kept telling me to leave, and the final straw was when you raised your hand to hit me. Your favor from the Lord is gone. You can see Caleb whenever you want, but we are finished."

He was silent for a few moments and said, "Wow, I had the caterpillar and when it turned into a butterfly, I let it go."

CHAPTER 2

Your Trash Is Someone Else's Treasure

It was just me and Caleb now. It had been a week since my husband last called to talk to Caleb. Caleb spent the weekends with his dad. He looked forward to seeing him, and I looked forward to some me time. Caleb's dad was really good with him and he loved Caleb, but he was very much still angry with me. We did the two-parent home for about one year until Caleb's father was evicted from his apartment. He had to move into a shelter until he was able to find an apartment. That meant Caleb would not be able to see him that often anymore. One day I noticed that a man, one of my neighbors who lived down the hall from me, was watching us when we came in and out of the apartment.

One morning, we were leaving out and my neighbor said, "Good morning Caleb. How are you?" and gave him a high five.

I was wondering how he knew Caleb, and immediately Caleb said, "Good morning, Mr. Sly."

Mr. Sly looked at me and said, "I see Caleb in the morning with his dad when he brings him home and I'm returning from my morning run."

I said, "Oh, okay. Nice to meet you," and we left. Later, I found out that Mr. Sly was the nice guy in the building who helped everybody out.

That evening, Caleb and I were coming into the building, and we ran into Mr. Sly. He said, "Good evening. I noticed you park your car around the corner in the lot, and it's dark out when you come home. When you are ready to come from the garage, just call me and I will walk around the corner to get you."

I said, "Okay. Thank you. That's very nice of you." I said to myself, *"It is dark when I come home, so I think I will take him up on his offer."* The next evening, I was coming home from Bible Study, and it was very late. Caleb was asleep, and I did not have enough strength to carry him all the way around the corner from the garage, so I called Mr. Sly, and he came right away to walk us home. We got to my door, I thanked him and went into the apartment. *"What a nice man,"* I thought.

I called my mom to let her know we arrived home, and she asked me, "Have you seen Caleb's dad?"

I said, "Not since he's been in the shelter."

She told me about her neighbor who was renting his basement apartment and asked did I think he would want to live in a basement.

I said, "I'm sure he wouldn't care because it's better than the shelter. At least he would get to see Caleb, and he would have his own place."

My mom called her neighbor and put in a good word, and he was able to move in that weekend. I picked him up from the shelter, and he moved into his one-room basement apartment. I noticed over the next few months that his health was getting really bad, and he had gained over a hundred pounds. After all, we didn't see him that much after he moved into the shelter. God laid it upon my mom's heart to feed him and look after him when she could. Because he couldn't get around like he used to due to the weight, he gave my mom a key to get into his apartment when she fixed him food.

Meanwhile, Mr. Sly and I became good friends. He was very helpful to me and Caleb. I would put my garbage outside the door so when I left, I could take it to the dumpster; but when I opened the door to leave, the garbage would be gone. I figured it was Mr. Sly because he was only two doors down, and besides, who else would it be? He always did things like that for me. He would bring my groceries from the car, walk us home at night, shovel my car out when it snowed, and he even bought me some cough medicine when I was sick.

My girlfriend came over that night, and I was telling her about Sly. She looked at me and said, "Really? You don't get it that he likes you?"

I said, "He does that for all the women in the building." She looked at me and shook her head. After she left, I thought about our conversation and said, "Maybe she's right." But I was still married, and I was not thinking about him like that. I did like the fact that he was a man of God and had some really good qualities of a good man. I did start to think that I should get a divorce because I knew I wanted to be married with a man that loved God, had his own relationship with God, and would love me and my son. On February 14, 2012, one year after filing, I was divorced and free indeed. After I left the courthouse on Valentine's Day, I went to the movies and took myself out to eat. I was happy.

CHAPTER 3

Is Sly My Boaz?

Boaz actually **means** "strength is within him" (bo = in him, az= strength)

Waiting for your **Boaz means** getting to know who you really are inside, what you're capable of, and what you're called to **do**. ...**Waiting** for your **Boaz means** preparation. It's a time to prepare for wifehood and pray for your future husband and yourself.

After two years of being single and working on me, I was ready to date again. At least my girlfriend and my sister were ready for me to date again. "How do you date when you don't have time to go out?" I would say to them. My girlfriend tried setting me up on dates all the time, but I would always cancel at the last minute. My girlfriend would get so mad at me, but I would ask her, "How are you going to set me up on a date and you don't have a man?" (I always laughed when I asked her this) and besides, I just didn't have time to go out. When Caleb went to his dad's apartment on the weekends, that was my me time. Who had time for a man?

Sly was still taking out my garbage, walking me home from the garage, and bringing my groceries upstairs from the car. He was my man, and he didn't even know it; I didn't know it. He was so nice, but I never saw him with a woman, and I never saw any women coming or going from his apartment. There I go being nosy; get you some business. LOL.

In 2011, the day before Thanksgiving, I was in my kitchen cooking a small feast and singing and dancing with myself. I heard the Lord say, "Go give him your phone number." I peeked out the kitchen door to make sure no one was in the house with me because I know that was not the voice of the Lord. I turned up my music and started dancing again. Again, I heard the Lord say, "Go give him your phone number."

I said, "Lord, you know I do not do that." When men asked for my phone number, I always gave them my sister's or my girlfriend's number. They would get so mad at me when I gave their numbers out to men who wanted my number. I figured they needed a man too. Why not help them out?

I heard the Lord a third time, so I wrote my phone number down on a piece of paper and marched my tore up looking self two doors down and knocked on Sly's door. I had a scarf on my head, t-shirt with food stains, and some raggedy sweatpants on. I said to myself, *"He told me to go give Sly my number. He didn't say change my clothes."*

Sly opened the door and I said, "Here's my phone number. You can call me whenever you want to talk."

His mouth dropped open, and he had this shocked look on his face like I was standing there naked. I said to myself, *"Close your mouth dude,"* and I walked away.

One hour later, there was a knock on my door. I went to see who it was, and it was Sly asking if I had any garbage to be taken down on his way out to work.

I said, "Yes, I do. I've been cooking all morning, and my garbage is full." Then I said, "Let me fix you some lunch."

He said, "You know how to cook?"

I turned my head around so quick and said, "Cook? No, I can burn bro!"

He laughed and said, "I would love to take some lunch. Thank you." He took his lunch, took my garbage, looked at me and smiled and said, "I'll talk to you later." Four hours later, Mr. Sly called me on his lunch break and thanked me for his lunch. Then he said, "You cook like you were born in the South."

We started talking on the phone almost every night after that. I was beginning to like Mr. Sly, but although I had started the divorce proceedings, I knew I was still legally married, so we stayed friends. We went to the movies from time to time. Caleb and I went to church with him on Family and Friends Day, and he would sit in the park with me while Caleb played. He was a man's man as the older generation described men who opened car doors, had respect for women, and were generally men with good characteristics. I must say I loved the fact that he had his own relationship with God. I continued to serve in

38

ministry faithfully and worked on myself emotionally, spiritually, and physically. My BFF Pastor Ieisha suggested that I attend New York School of the Bible. She took some classes there and knew it would be great for me. She always saw greatness in me and pushed me to be better. I started going to the Bible School, going to the gym, and working on myself emotionally.

I asked God to show me myself, show me what I did or did not do in my twenty-year marriage, so I could work on not repeating the same behavior. I didn't want to bring my old self into a new relationship or a new marriage. I understood that marriage was work, and I wanted to be emotionally whole going into the next marriage. I needed to be emotionally whole and complete without a man, while working on my relationship with God. As He began to mold and shape me into the woman of God that He designed me to be, I had to give God a complete yes. I was preparing for Boaz while working on me.

I was sitting in class talking to my girlfriend who was attending the Bible school too, and this tall handsome guy walked into the class and asked me if the seat next to me was taken. I said, "No, you can sit there." So he did, but during the entire class, I caught him staring at me. I said to myself, *"Here we go. You cute, but I know you are not my Boaz."*

After class, the guy, whose name was Thomas, asked if he could have my phone number. I said no and walked away.

My girlfriend said, "You are so cold! You're going to be old and alone if you keep saying no to every guy that asks for your phone number."

I said, "That's not my Boaz. So why waste my time?" She rolled her eyes, shook her head, and followed me onto the elevator.

The following Saturday, Thomas walked into the class, handed me a bag and said, "I was thinking about you all week. I bought you a muffin and a coffee. I saw you eating one last Saturday."

I said, "No thank you. But thank you for the gesture."

Immediately, my girlfriend said, "I'll take it." I looked at her with this *'I'm going to kill you'* look, and she said, What?"

After class, Thomas asked if he could walk me to the train station and I said, "No thanks. I'm walking with a friend. Have a great time at church tomorrow," and walked away. My friend sucked her teeth and walked ahead of me. The following Saturday, on the train going to school, I was praying Thomas would not be in class and definitely without any more gifts. As soon as I walked off the elevator, who was standing there with a huge box? You guessed it. Thomas. He looked at me and said, "I have some gifts for you."

I immediately got an attitude and said, "I told you I do not want any gifts."

Thomas replied, "Please... just look in the box."

I stood there and guess who started pulling items out of the box? You guessed again -- my girlfriend. The box had hats, socks, scarves, candy, peanuts, and all sorts of things. I asked Thomas, "Where did you get these things from?"

He said, "I work at a church, and they allow me to take whatever I need after the homeless take what they need."

Now you know I had a serious attitude. Right? I said, "How in the world are you going to bring me gifts that were given to you?"

He said, "I wanted to show you how much I like you."

I said, "I like gifts wrapped up with wrapping paper or in a bag with some colorful tissue paper."

41

He looked at me and said, "God told me you were my wife."

I looked at him and said, "You need a green card. Don't you?"

He said, "No, I'm a citizen."

I replied, "I was just checking because you only met me two weeks ago, and now I'm your wife." I turned around and walked into class and sat down between two other students so he wouldn't sit next to me.

My girlfriend walked over to me and said, "Why do you treat Thomas so bad?"

I said, "You marry him. God told me to prepare myself for Boaz, nothing less, and definitely not someone looking to get a green card." Thomas ignored me for the rest of the semester. Every time I saw him, he was talking to a different woman. I guess he was still trying to find his Ruth.

Mr. Sly was still hanging in there. We became good friends, but I think we both wanted more. We started dating in April, and that's when I decided to bring Caleb around Sly. Caleb knew Sly, but he didn't spend any time with him. Since we decided to try the dating thing, I had to make sure Caleb felt comfortable around him and liked him. If Caleb didn't like him, it was definitely not going to work and would be over really quick. Saturday, we all went to the movies and then the sporting goods store.

Sly picked up a basketball and said, "Come on little man. Let's shoot some hoops."

After watching them play for thirty minutes, Caleb sat down next to me sweating and breathing heavy. When he caught his breath, he said, "I like him." He got up to finish playing ball. That was a relief. One down and three more introductions to go.

Introduction number two, I called and invited Sly, my BFF Pastor Ieisha, and a couple other of my friends to go out to a stage play with me the following Saturday. After the play, we all went to dinner. We arrived at the restaurant, and Sly's eyes immediately got big because he realized that he was the only man with five women. I laughed to myself and said, *"If he survives this dinner, he is definitely going to be okay for the next two introductions."*

During dinner, Sly was having a conversation with Ieisha while my other friends were staring and acting awkward; but I knew I sat him next to the right one, Ieisha. She was talking to Sly and looking at me smiling. When the bill came, Sly didn't hesitate to take the bill and pay it without asking for any money from any of us. Ieisha leaned over and said, "He's the one. That's Boaz."

We laughed. Introduction number three, dinner with my family. Sly picked me up, and we went to my parents' house. We got to my parents' house and everyone had already decided to go to New York for dinner. We arrived at the restaurant, and I could tell Sly was a little nervous. My sister was being nosy and asking all kinds of questions. He answered her, and she seemed to be satisfied. After about an hour, my parents gave me the nod which meant they liked him, especially my dad. You know a man knows another man.

Dinner was going well, and I was being my pleasant and funny self. We got home and Sly told me that he didn't know that I was so funny and the life of the party. He thought I was serious all the time because I was a minister, and he had never seen me laughing and joking so much.

I laughed and said, "I wear many hats to balance my life, but remember I'm a woman first."

He said, "Yes you are, and if I had met you twenty years ago..."

My mouth dropped open. I was hanging on every word, and then he changed the subject.

Really dude? We were getting serious, and he still had one last introduction, my pastor. I was not looking forward to that meeting. Sly was very quiet, meek, and laid back. I often wondered if he was strong enough for me. I had never seen him angry, lose his temper, or yell, so of course I wondered if he was strong or passive because I didn't want to be the man in the relationship and the one to make all the decisions. I told Sly I think we should fast and pray for seven days to see what God is saying concerning our relationship, and he agreed. After the seven days, God spoke to me in a dream, but I wasn't sure God spoke to Sly, and I was not going to be the first to say anything about it. Also, he still hadn't met my pastor yet.

The following Sunday, Sly came to my church to meet my pastor and my church family. Pastor asked to meet with Sly after church. After their meeting, my pastor said, "He's a good man, and he's a strong man with a good character."

After church, me, Sly and Caleb went out to dinner. When we arrived home, Sly carried Caleb from the car to our apartment and put him to bed. We sat in the living room and talked about our day. Sly told me he wanted to tell me what God

45

said to him during our fast, so I sat back and waited for him to start talking. He explained to me that his intentions were to transfer his job to the Veterans Hospital in South Carolina and retire alone as soon as an opening became available. He never thought he would meet someone like me.

He said, "I thought about our 14-year age difference, and it scared me because I don't want you to have to take care of me if I got sick. I don't want to be a burden on you. It wouldn't be fair. You already have a child, and you've been through enough. But God told me to look at all the scriptures I could find on fear and recite them until I memorized them. God told me that He is giving me the desire of my heart that I forgot about and thought He forgot about too. God told me you were my wife months ago, but I was scared. I am no longer operating in fear. You are my wife. Will you marry me?"

I started dating Sly in April of 2012, and he proposed to me in August of 2012. Our wedding date was set for May 4, 2013. We were planning a beautiful wedding, and I was so happy. My wedding was everything I didn't get with my first marriage that I deserved. May 4th finally arrived, and I was overjoyed at how God was blessing us.

He gave me my heart's desire. Sly stayed at his best man's house the night before, and I stayed at my mom's house with my bridesmaids. The house was so busy with all the women getting their hair done and their makeup done. Everyone looked so beautiful. All of a sudden, my best friend came running in the house and said, "Girl, your ex-husband is outside with grocery bags talking to some of your family members and friends."

I said, "Why in the world would he be outside on my wedding day? Did you guys make sure it was safe for me to leave?" I ran to the window, and my ex-husband was outside of my mom's house on my wedding day. I couldn't believe what I was seeing.

My aunt asked me, "Why is he outside?"

I said, "He lives next door." We turned towards each other and shook our heads. I did my best to wait for him to leave, but he wouldn't. I was not going to be late for my wedding, so I said, "Let's go and get in the car."

The chauffeur grabbed my arm and escorted me down the steps. My eight bridesmaids, three flower girls, and two bride criers followed me. I didn't look to the right or the left. I looked straight ahead, got into my Excalibur and drove off to go marry my BOAZ.

I didn't want the night to end, but it had to. The next day, we left on a cruise to Bermuda for seven days. When we returned, Caleb and I moved into Sly's apartment, and we started saving for a house. Almost two years later, on March 6, 2015, we purchased our first home six houses down from my parents. Two weeks later, I was drinking a cup of coffee on my sunporch, and I noticed a man watching me. I stood up to get a closer look, and it was my ex-husband watching me as he walked to the train station.

I immediately sat down and thought, *"Wow, isn't that something? You threw me and my son out, and now you are walking past my house because you didn't want the blessings and favor God gave you."*

One year later, Caleb came home and told me his dad was moving.

"Again?" I said, and Caleb responded, "Yes. He's moving across the street from my school which is only two blocks away." All I could do was laugh. I guess it was good for Caleb because he loved being with his dad, and I wanted him to have a healthy relationship with his dad. He moved into his apartment and gave Caleb a key to come and go as he pleased. When he got out of school, he could just go directly across the street.

One year later, Caleb's dad completely stopped coming outside because he could not get around due to his weight gain, and this prevented him from being able to go up and down the stairs. Caleb was a big help to his dad. He would go to the store for his dad, help clean the apartment, and make sure he got the mail every day. Caleb was his "Buddy" as his dad would say every time he saw Caleb. Caleb spent the weekends with his dad, and he would check on his dad in the mornings before he went to school.

Caleb loved his dad, and his dad adored him. The weight was taking a toll on his body, and it seemed as if he was giving up on life. It had been almost two years since he'd been out of his apartment, and I couldn't help but wonder how a man with so much life ahead of him could just give up so easily. When I met him, he was so athletic, in great shape, had a great sense of humor, and he loved life. I thought about all the years we spent together and wondered why he gave up on the marriage so easily as if 20 years meant nothing to him. I thought about the words he would say to me every anniversary, and when he said this comment to me, he would laugh so hysterically. Every August 4th, he would say, "My twenty-year sentence is almost up. I'm almost free."

And you know what? He spoke that phrase for twenty years, and on August 4th, on our twentieth anniversary, his sentence was up. He was a free man; his jail sentence, as he called it, was up. He spoke the death of our marriage for twenty years as a joke, but his words had power over his life.

"The tongue has the power of life and death, and those who love it will eat its fruit. He who finds a wife finds what is good and receives favor from the Lord." (Proverbs 18:21-22)

SLY IS MY BOAZ!!

CHAPTER 4

Life After The Honeymoon

We had just arrived home from Bermuda. We enjoyed our honeymoon immensely and didn't want to come back, but we had to. Bermuda was beautiful, colorful, romantic, and too short. We needed more than seven days. We opened the door to the apartment, and gifts were everywhere in Sly's apartment. Wow! It was our apartment now. We unwrapped all the gifts and were so thankful for all the beautiful gifts from our family and friends.

Caleb came home, and he was so excited to see us. The first thing he said was, "Hey Daddy Sly."

I looked at Sly. He had this big grin on his face. He walked over to Caleb, gave him a high five and said, "What's up man?" I thought that was the cutest thing I ever heard. Caleb came up with that name all on his own. It was getting late, so we all got ready for bed because we had to go to work and school the next day.

I couldn't wait to get to work to show my coworkers my pictures from my honeymoon. They were guests at my wedding and couldn't wait to see the pictures either. On my lunch break, I marched my little happy, married self over to human resources to change my last name. I was smiling so hard, my face started to hurt. I said to myself, *"Stop acting like a crazy person, and stop smiling like you just won something."* Love has a way of making you smile from the inside out.

It was very important for me to do things differently in my second marriage. I made it my number one priority to communicate with my husband no matter what. If we had a disagreement, we would talk it out and not be angry, and we definitely would not get angry with each other and walk around the house and not talk to one another. I promised myself we would live, laugh, and love on purpose. Sly works second shift and I work first shift, so we would do most of our talking in the morning before I went to work or in the evening when he came home from work. I would take a nap, wake up about one hour before Sly would come home, take a shower, and be up and ready to talk when he came home. I always had his food ready for him on the stove or in the microwave, but he ate something light and took his dinner to work for lunch. Sly would make my breakfast and lunch every morning while I was getting dressed for work. He would bring my breakfast to me, sit it on a tray, and say, "Babe, your breakfast is ready."

I never had a man make me breakfast every morning. I was loving it and enjoying it. I didn't know what to do with myself. I just prayed it wouldn't stop because I was getting used to being pampered, and I was definitely bragging to my friends at work.

Six months later, I was still getting the royal treatment. One year later, the same thing. Two years later, I was just spoiled. He was taking care of me the way I take care of others. He was very caring and attentive to my feelings and made sure that I didn't need anything. If I was sick, I didn't have to worry about cooking, cleaning, or Caleb. He took care of the house and made sure Caleb was okay. He got Caleb ready for school, dropped him off, and picked him up so I could stay in the bed and rest. He literally brought me my medicine, my breakfast, lunch, and dinner, and he never complained.

Whenever I was sick in my first marriage, I still had to cook, clean, and take care of Caleb. I just couldn't believe how caring Sly was. Sly's love language is definitely, Acts of Service. I would say my love language is Words of Affirmation, Receiving Gifts, and Physical Touch. (The 5 Love Languages: The Secret to Love that Lasts by Gary Chapman)

After getting over the flu and getting my strength back, I went out with my girlfriends. I told them about my experience with Sly when I was sick. I wanted them to understand their husband's love language and stop getting upset with their spouses because they don't express the same love language; but understand that we all have our own love language, and we must get to know what our spouse's language is.

There are five love languages: *Words of Affirmation, Acts of Service, Receiving Gifts, Quality Time, and Physical Touch.*

I believe just by knowing this simple tool, it will help a lot of marriages. Marriage is work, but if you take time to understand your spouse, it becomes a little easier.

A couple of weeks later, I was sick again. This time, the over the counter medicine was not working. I told my husband, "Something is wrong, and I need to go to the doctor."

He took me to the doctor the next day and my doctor took some bloodwork and ran every test he could think of. He told me he would call me when the blood work came back. Two days later, the doctor called and asked if I could come into the office. I told him I would come to his office the next morning before work and he said, "I need to see you right away."

I swallowed really hard and said, "I will see you in twenty minutes."

I arrived at the doctor's office. The nurse escorted me into room number 3 and said, "The doctor will be right with you." She walked out and closed the door. I began to panic and think of all the things that could be wrong with me. Then, I decided to pray and calm myself down.

The doctor knocked, opened the door, came in and sat down. He said, "Mrs. Jones, I'm sorry to tell you that you have type two diabetes and need to take insulin right away. Your sugar is 365."

I saw his mouth moving, but I didn't hear anything after he said diabetes. Tears started coming down my face. My eyes got blurry. I couldn't believe what I was hearing. He gave me some tissue to wipe my face and told me he knew it was difficult to hear, but he needed to give me a shot of insulin to lower my blood sugar, and he would teach me how to give myself the insulin.

He said, "The good thing is type two diabetes is treatable if you follow all the directions to help lower your AIC."

I asked him, "What's the difference between the two? How do you even become diabetic?"

He said, "People with type 1 diabetes don't produce insulin. People with type 2 diabetes don't respond to insulin as well as they should." Then he said, "Type 2 diabetes develops when the body becomes resistant to insulin or when the pancreas is unable to produce enough insulin."

The doctor gave me all my directions, my prescriptions, and sent me upstairs to the dietician. After an hour, I called my job and requested a personal day.

Then I called Sly and told him everything. I just cried on the phone. As I sobbed in his ear he said, "Don't cry. I'm on my way home. We will get through this together."

Sly came home. We talked, and I was so upset. I fell asleep. When I woke up, Sly was laying across my legs sleep. I looked at him and thanked God for this man. The next few days, I was sick because of the medicine, and my body had to get used to the insulin and adjust to my new diet. Sly knew how to read my body language better than I did and was able to look at me and tell me when my sugar was too high or when it was too low.

Sly was such a big help to me. He talked to doctors at his job to get a better understanding about diabetes and the different symptoms you have when your sugar levels are high or low. He changed his diet and ate only what I was able to eat. He took all the snacks out of the house and replaced them with sugar free snacks, sugar free ice cream, and we ate no fried foods.

I couldn't believe this man gave up fried chicken for me. He was such a huge help to me. He helped me get through this transition as if he had diabetes. I looked at Sly and said, "Look who has to take care of who. And you were worried about our age difference and if you were to get sick how I would have to take care of you. Look who's taking care of who."

He looked at me and said, "I'll always take care of you." He has an inner strength big enough for me and him. Sly is truly my Boaz!!

Eight years later, he has not changed. Sly is still taking care of me and Caleb. He's teaching Caleb how to be a man and how to take care of me too. God has truly blessed us with someone who is caring, selfless, compassionate, genuinely a good person, and who has great characteristics, but most of all, he loves us.

CHAPTER 5

Forgiving Beyond The Grave

On September 16, 2018, Caleb came home from his dad's house crying hysterically and repeating, "Is it true? Is it true?"

I didn't understand what was going on, and I asked Caleb, "What happened? Why are you crying?"

He looked in my eyes and said, "Am I adopted?" I was so shocked and upset at the same time. I thought, *"How dare you tell him he's adopted without my permission or without us discussing it?"*

I started to cry, and I said, "Yes." Caleb began to cry even harder, and so did I. I told Caleb to calm down and go into the house, and that I would be in to talk to him in five minutes. I was so upset and hurt. All I could do was sit in my car and cry and scream, *"How dare he hurt me and my son like this?"* I had so many thoughts running through my head. I started talking to God asking Him, "How do I tell him like this?"

I called my husband crying hysterically on the phone. He kept saying, "Baby what's wrong? What's going on?" I finally stopped crying and told him what happened. He told me to stop crying, pray, and go talk to Caleb. He said, "You have to straighten out the mess your ex-husband has caused." Then he said, "Go and talk to Caleb. He needs the truth right now."

I got out of my car and walked into the house. Caleb was sitting on the couch crying. I sat next to him, and we both cried. I finally got up the nerve to speak and I said, "Yes, you are adopted. You are my nephew and my brother is your biological father, but I am your mother. I've been with you since the day you were born. You are my son, my child."

We hugged and cried some more. Caleb had this blank look on his face. I asked him what was wrong, and he said, "I can't believe he's my father. Wow, I can't believe it."

I asked him, "Why do you say it like that?"

He replied, "I just can't believe he's my father." I don't think he was happy my brother was his father. We got ourselves together, and we began to talk. Caleb had so many questions, and I was finally ready to answer them. The first question he asked was, "Where is my real mother?"

That was a slap in the face for me, but I had to understand that he needed to ask these questions, and I had to understand that it wasn't to be mean. I told him that his biological mother passed away during labor, and I only met her one time and didn't know much about her. All I know is she had complications during labor due to asthma. He was silent for a moment; then he asked a series of questions, and I answered him. I wanted to make sure Caleb was okay, so I told him he could ask me whatever he wanted, and I would answer him honestly.

I asked him was he upset, and he said, "I'm upset at how I found out. Why didn't you tell me?"

I explained to him how I wanted to tell him, but my brother begged me not to. I told Caleb, "I didn't want you to feel rejected if he didn't want to talk to you or be around you."

I told him I was going to tell him, but I wanted to make sure he was mature enough to handle it; and even though he was 12 years old, I didn't think he was ready, and I guess I wanted to protect him.

I asked him if he wanted me to tell my brother that he knew he was his biological father, and he replied, "No, I do not want him to know that I know he's my father."

So, I told him I would not say a word. I explained to him how his family dynamic hasn't changed because he's adopted. I was his mother, my mom is still his grandmother, my sister is still his aunty, and his cousins are still his cousins.

I asked Caleb if he wanted to tell the family and he said, "I only want to tell my grandmother." And so, we only told my mom that Caleb knew he was adopted. Even though I was furious with Caleb's dad, my ex-husband, I felt a little relieved that Caleb knew; but I was so angry with my ex-husband, and I couldn't wait to call him.

After our talk and after Caleb went to his room, I called his dad and gave him a piece of my mind. I asked him, "Why would you tell Caleb he's adopted the way you did? You had no right to tell him without discussing it with me first! You did that to get back at me because I don't want you. God will not allow you to hurt us. If you wanted to get back at me, hurt me, not my son! What you did was mean and vicious, but I won't let your hatred for me hurt my son."

He finally responded and said, "I only told him because he asked."

I said, "Why would Caleb just ask if he's adopted out of nowhere?" There was a silence on the phone.

I hung up the phone and went into Caleb's room to talk to him about what just happened. I asked Caleb did he bring up the subject or did his dad. He said his dad had been saying things to him. I asked him, "What things?"

He said, "Remember when I was in trouble at school?"

I said, "Yes."

He said his dad was talking to him about his behavior and he said, "You're just like your dad."

I said, "What did he say?" Caleb repeated what I was scared to hear. Now I was really mad because who says that to a child and doesn't think it would bring confusion? Now the puzzle pieces were coming together, and I was getting angrier by the minute. I was angry. Caleb was angry. We both were angry with his dad. I asked Caleb if he wanted to talk to his dad and ask him any questions he needed answered, but he said no.

I really needed to pray because if God was coming back that night, I would have missed Him. I'm telling you; I was fuming mad and didn't want to talk to my ex-husband ever again.

Day two, September 17, 2018, I asked Caleb did he talk to his dad and he said no.

I told Caleb he had to forgive his father and he asked me, "Are you mad with him?"

I said, "Yes I am, but I forgive him, and you have to do the same." We have to pray and ask God to help us forgive him, and you should call him and tell him you're not upset anymore."

But he said no, and I didn't force him. Day three, September 18, 2018, I asked Caleb if he called his dad and he said no. Again, I told Caleb not to be angry and to call his father, but he was not ready, and I didn't push the issue. Day four, September 19, 2018, I decided not to ask again and let Caleb work it out on his own with his dad. I didn't have to talk to my ex-husband because he and Caleb had their own relationship. I only got involved when I needed to.

The next day, I received a phone call. The person on the other end asked if my name was

Tisha and did I have a son named Caleb. I said, "Yes. How may I help you?"

The woman on the phone said, "I live next door to your ex-husband. I found your phone number on an old prescription bottle in his apartment."

I asked if everything was okay and she said, "I'm sorry to tell you. Your ex-husband passed away this afternoon."

I couldn't believe what I just heard. I began to cry and said, "How am I going to tell my son his father is dead? Oh God! Help me."

The woman said, "I'm so sorry."

I told the woman on the phone that I would come around the corner as soon as I could. I called my husband and told him what happened.

He immediately said, "I'm on my way home."

I hung up with him and called my mom crying hysterically. She was so scared and kept asking me what was wrong, but I couldn't speak. Two minutes later, my mom was ringing my doorbell. Thank God she was down the street. I opened the door and told her what happened. She was shocked and speechless. She kept telling me to stop crying, calm down, and tell her what happened.

I got myself together and told her exactly what the woman on the phone said. I kept asking my mom how was I going to tell Caleb his father has passed away. I couldn't believe he was gone. I was angry with him, but I never thought he would not be here to see Caleb grow up. The first thing that came to my mind was, *"I hope Caleb decided to call his dad because I don't want him to feel guilty about being upset and not reaching out to him, and now he's gone."*

Caleb was still in school, and I immediately tried to call Caleb to make sure he came straight home. Caleb had keys to his dad's apartment, and he would go over to his place after school because his school was directly across the street from his dad's place. Caleb answered the phone, and I told him to make sure he came straight home and not to stop at his dad's house, but to come straight home. Caleb walked through the door and immediately asked me what was wrong. I think he was able to feel my spirit and saw how sad I was.

As soon as my husband came home, I told Caleb to finish his homework and that me and grandma would be right back. My mom drove us around the corner to my ex-husband's apartment. We walked in the apartment, and thank God, the coroner had already picked up the body. My mother had a key too, because she would fix my ex-husband food and take it to him every week because he was confined to his apartment. My ex-husband's neighbor and some friends were already in the apartment when we arrived.

I greeted everyone and immediately asked, "What happened?"

My ex-husband's colleague said he tried to call him all morning because he was supposed to go to the grocery store for him. When he didn't answer, he decided to come to the apartment and check on him, and when he didn't answer the door, he went next door to the neighbor because the neighbor also had a key. His friend found him in the bed unresponsive.

I was praying and so happy he didn't suffer. We left the building, and I kept praying and asking God, "How do I tell Caleb his father is gone?"

When I got home, I went into my bedroom and cried on my husband's lap because all I kept thinking was, *"I can't tell Caleb tonight, because I don't know how to tell a 12-year-old he will never see his dad again."*

The more I thought about it, the more I cried. I was hurting for my son and trying to protect him at the same time. I cried myself to sleep on my husband's lap, and he just held me and prayed. God has truly blessed me with a wonderful man of God.

The next morning, I got up early and called Caleb's school to tell them the news and to let them know Caleb would not be in school. They completely understood and excused him for the day or two days if we needed it. Caleb woke up about ten o'clock, came into our bedroom and said, "I'm not going to school today?"

I said, "I need to tell you something. Come here."

He looked at my face and, in my eyes, and he knew something was wrong. He could tell I had been crying. He walked over to me and stood in front of me. I opened my mouth, and no words came out. Only tears from my eyes and I began to cry out loud.

Caleb was getting nervous and asked me to please tell him what was wrong.

I stopped crying and said, "Your dad passed away honey. I'm so sorry."

Caleb looked at me with a look I will never forget. He looked like he saw a ghost but couldn't run. After a couple of minutes, Caleb fell into my lap and said, "But I didn't get to say goodbye."

When I heard those words, my heart sank into my stomach. I began to hold and rock my child until he stopped crying. Caleb looked into my eyes and said, "Who's going to take care of my dad now?"

I said, "We are. We will take care of everything." Caleb climbed into my bed, and we cried and talked until we both felt better. I just wanted to squeeze the pain out of him.

I knew I had to make sure I took care of the funeral arrangements because I promised my son we would. I began to plan some things out, but I felt myself getting angry because my ex-husband created emotional trauma with me and my son. He was gone and I had to fix it. How do I bury my ex while being angry? I forgave him, but I was still angry. Can you forgive and still be angry? I needed God to help me forgive him because I couldn't do it on my own.

I needed to show my son that you have to forgive even when it hurts, because the forgiveness is for you, not them. I prayed and I prayed for God to heal the hurt that my ex-husband caused and to teach me to forgive him. How do I pick up the pieces and put them back together now, plan a funeral, and take care of my son's emotional state at the same time?

I asked my son did he want to help with the decisions because he knew what his father liked. As I began to call and make funeral arrangements, Caleb would help here and there. I didn't ask him. I just told him, "You can do what you want, when you feel like it."

After everything was finalized, Pastor Ieisha stepped in and helped me with the obituary. I gathered all the photos I had from an old photo album book and some pictures that were in my ex-husband's apartment. I asked Caleb if there was anything he wanted to keep from his dad's apartment, and he said no.

I said, "Are you sure?"

He walked to a closet, opened it up, and grabbed an 8x10 picture of his dad when he was younger. Caleb turned to me and said, "That's all I want. Can we go now?"

We walked towards the door and never returned. As I was writing out the obituary, Caleb walked into my study and said, "His favorite color was blue. Can we all wear blue to the funeral?"

I said, "Of course, we can. Is there anything else you want?

Before he left the room, he turned to me and said, "I would like to have yellow flowers also."

As soon as he left, I cried because I thought it was so thoughtful and brave of him. I was so proud of him and hurting for him at the same time.

September 26, 2018, the day of the funeral, Caleb had on his blue suit. My husband wore his blue suit, and I wore my blue dress because this is what my son wanted. He wanted all of us to wear his dad's favorite color. We walked out the door and headed to the funeral home, and I said to God, "We need you today like never before."

The service was beautiful. The yellow flowers stood out in the funeral home. All his family and friends came to say goodbye. I was worried because Caleb only cried once when the officiant said his father always said, "Hey Buddy," when he saw Caleb.

After the service, we all went out to eat and enjoyed each other's company. I looked at my son and asked God to help me help him. The next morning, Caleb climbed into my bed and said, "I didn't say goodbye."

I hugged my son and told him, "Your dad knew you loved him, and you have to forgive yourself for not talking to him before he passed. Only God knew he would leave us, and it is not your burden to take on." That day, I called a grief counselor for me and my son.

CHAPTER 6

Purposely Positioned

Serving in ministry was preparing me for the shoes God had ordained for me to walk in before I was called. I believe serving in ministry helps you see who you are, and it allows you to work on you before the elevation. I also believe that God puts people in your life to help you move into the next level of ministry. Pastor Ieisha was one of those people. She didn't allow me to quit, she didn't allow me to walk in fear about my next level, and she definitely didn't bring any soda or chips when I was having a pity party.

Pastor Ieisha told me the truth and then said, "Let's get on with it. You have too much to do for the Kingdom."

Pastor Ieisha understood my level of serving in ministry because she served in ministry the same way. I had to adjust my serving in ministry with my new role as a wife. I personally believe that the hierarchy for serving in ministry is God, family, and then ministry. I never want to neglect my family because I'm serving in ministry more than I'm serving at home.

There's a balance that you need in order to be successful in life and ministry. If you don't know how to balance family and ministry, you have to ask God for help. Sly has always had his own relationship with God, but he has a different view on serving in ministry than I do, and once we got married, I had to be sensitive to the Holy Spirit when I scheduled my time to serve. I still served on Sundays, but I didn't stay three hours after service anymore. I went home to be with my son and husband, so we could eat dinner together.

I scheduled the single women to serve more hours than the married women, so our families would not be neglected. Our first ministry is to our family. You cannot be successful in ministry, neglect your home, and expect for your home not to lack or suffer from your absence. I try to show my husband and son that they are just as important as the church, and I will always choose them first.

After being separated for three years, I had spent most of my time in ministry and serving, and now that I was married again, I had to adjust. My husband understood the importance of me serving in ministry more than I gave him credit for. Sly came to me and said, "I know God has called you to ministry, and I would never get in the way of that. Do not change your schedule for me. I would never get in the way of God's plan and purpose for you. I'm here to help you move into your purpose, not to be a hinderance."

I said, *"Wow. I really underestimated one of the reasons God put him in my life."* It was not just for us, but for ministry as well. My first marriage was such a hinderance to my ministry. I just assumed I had to be very careful about the time I spent in church and serving, so I didn't repeat the same issues. I realized that without sitting down and talking to Sly about how he felt, it wasn't fair to think he would be the same. Then, I remembered when a prophet came to our church anniversary. He told me that the Lord said that the next husband is for ministry. After coming out of a twenty-year marriage, I didn't want to hear anything about another husband. So, I guess instead of writing down my prophecy like I usually did, I took that prophecy and stored it away because I heard the words "next husband."

The next Sunday, I had to serve a visiting pastor who was the guest speaker for our Women's Day Service. I prepared dinner Saturday night and made sure Caleb and Sly had everything they needed when they went home after service. I arrived home about two hours after Sly and Caleb. When I got out of my car to walk into the house, Sly was right there to take my bags out of the car and escort me into the house.

Sly said, "I'm going to make you a bath. I'll put your food in the microwave, so your food will be ready when you get out of the tub and put your pajamas on."

I looked at him, started walking up the stairs and said, "Who is this man? He is truly sent by God."

It was a little scary because I always had to argue when I got home when I had to stay late to serve. Now I didn't, and it felt good.

I was free to serve without worrying about my serving causing controversy and having to argue when I got home. God has given me someone who understands my call to ministry. God has Purposely Positioned Sly in our lives, and I didn't really understand it until God showed me his place in ministry with me.

Even though Sly came from a different denomination and was not serving in ministry the way I was, he understands the call that God has on my life, and he supports me. He makes serving easier for me. Now I understand that God will not give you a spouse that will be a hinderance to your ministry. I believe that your marriage represents the Kingdom. Now that doesn't mean that you will not go through things, but if your spouse was chosen by God, God will help you through the hard times.

It was time for me to prepare for school. Fall semester was starting in a couple of weeks, and I was excited to go. Saturday morning arrived, and I was up and ready to catch the train when Sly walked in the bedroom and said, "You ready? Let's go." Sly was already up, dressed, and ready to go.

I asked him, "Where are you going so early?"

He said, "I'm going to New York to school with you."

I said, "You're going to take a class?"

He said, "No, I'm not letting you go to New York alone." Sly got up every Saturday for one year, sat on a bench outside of my classroom, waited for me for two hours, and never complained.

I was so overwhelmed at how God Purposely Positioned this man of God in my life to be such an integral part in helping me with my son and ministry. I thanked God every day. At my graduation, I told my husband, "You earned this diploma too."

I enrolled in Lancaster Bible College to earn my Bachelor of Arts in Biblical Studies. While taking my first online course, I was so overwhelmed with the amount of time it took to complete my assignments, juggle ministry, work, and be a wife and mother, but I knew I couldn't give up.

One Friday evening, my husband came home, walked into my study, and saw me crying. He said, "What's the matter?"

I told him I was falling behind in my schoolwork because my laptop was old and not compatible. I continued to cry, and I said to God, "I can't fail before I begin. Please help me figure this out."

I woke up Saturday morning exhausted from the night before. Sly walked into the bedroom with my breakfast like he did every morning and said, "After you finish eating, get dressed because I'm taking you somewhere."

I said, "Okay babe. I'll be dressed in thirty minutes."

But he knew that meant one hour. One hour and thirty minutes later, we pulled into the parking lot of a computer store. As we walked in, Sly went straight to the back to the laptops and asked the salesman, "What brand is the best?"

He replied, "Apple MacBook, of course."

Sly looked at me and said, "Pick out what you want."

I began to cry. I hugged him so tight and said, "You never stop amazing me."

Sly looked me in the eyes and said, "I want you to succeed."

God Purposely Positioned this man in my life. Twenty years of marriage and I never had this much support. He was not jealous, he was not selfish, and he wanted the best for me. Sly was being used by God to heal past hurts and disappointments. God was showing me that He hand-picked Sly just for me and Purposely Positioned us to glorify God in our marriage and ministry.

Sly's selflessness made ministry so much more comfortable for me. I was able to attend leadership conferences and women's retreats and not worry about Caleb. Sly would use his vacation days to stay with Caleb when I went away. I felt so free to serve in ministry like never before. It felt good to have help. Sly always encouraged me to attend different types of conferences. He would tell me, "You have to invest in yourself."

I loved the way he cared about me and the things that made me happy. I never had anyone that treated me the way I treated others. It was like God was showing me His love through a man – the man He picked for me. He's not perfect, but he is perfect for me. He takes care of me, and I take care of him.

We started serving in ministry together. We traveled with our pastor to outside preaching engagements, conferences, and retreats. Two years later, my pastor had a meeting with the leadership and told us he was resigning from ministry. I was sad, confused, and lost because I didn't know where we would wind up or even what ministry we should attend.

We decided to fast and get direction from God because we couldn't just go anywhere and needed to be under the right leadership and pastor. Two weeks after my pastor resigned, we were still waiting on a word from God, and until we received a word, we decided to visit a local church near our home on the following Sunday. I felt a little out of place because I have never not been in church or serving in ministry, so it was a little hard for me to not have a church home.

One month later and still no word from God, I was getting a little down in my spirit and wanted to stay home; but I felt a push in my spirit to get out of bed, get dressed, and go to church. We got dressed and went to a church in our neighborhood, and on that particular Sunday, they had a guest speaker. When the pastor introduced the visiting pastor, she also told the congregation that the guest pastor would be speaking for the next six Sundays while she was out on maternity leave.

During the service, the Lord spoke to me and said, "Give your ministry resume to the visiting Bishop."

I said, "What is a ministry resume?" and God said, "Write down everything you have done in your previous ministry, all the trainings you facilitated, and all the ministries you served on, and give it to the visiting Bishop next Sunday."

I was obedient and did what the Lord said. I called my former pastor and shared with him what the Lord told me to do. My former pastor said, "I will write you a character and ministry letter for the Bishop as well because this is God, and He is connecting you to your next pastor."

I knew this was God Purposely Positioning me and my family for our next ministry. The following Sunday as I was leaving the sanctuary, I went up to the Bishop, introduced myself, and gave him my ministry resume and the letter from my former pastor. I said, "God told me to give you my ministry resume."

He took the letter and said, "Thank you. God bless you."

CHAPTER 7

Elder-Elect

Six Sundays later, my family and I attended the Bishop's church, and we've been there ever since. After fasting and praying for over three months, God released me and my family to join the ministry. After one month of sitting and getting to know the ministry, I was given the opportunity to be the newly assigned President of the Women's Ministry, which I really was excited about.

Since I already had a women's book club that I started about three years prior in my home, I was excited to introduce the book club to the ministry. I had so many ideas and plans I wanted to share with the women, but it was not easy coming into a new ministry and getting the women on board. While I was planning a yearly calendar for the women's ministry, Sly was in training to serve as Bishop's Adjutant which I thought was very fitting for him. He was loyal, mature, faithful to the ministry, a confidant, and a tither. I was so happy to see Sly serving, but it felt so weird for me not to be serving as an Adjutant because I had served in that capacity for so long. I realized that I was so comfortable with serving in the same role, but God was trying to shift me into my new position.

My new ministry also meant a new mind shift. This meant Purposely Positioning myself for the next level that was way overdue according to Bishop.

I prayed and asked God why was there so much resistance. The Lord replied, "I Purposely Positioned you in this ministry. Don't worry about who is not willing. Work with those who are, and the rest will follow."

That word hit me like a ton of bricks. After that, I focused on the things I could change and prayed about the things I couldn't. After serving under Bishop for one year, God spoke to me and said I needed to have a talk with Bishop and tell him what God had been telling and showing me in dreams about my next level in ministry. My husband and I met with Bishop for breakfast, and as I began to tell Bishop what God had been saying to me, it was a confirmation of what God had been saying to Bishop as well.

After our meeting, Bishop set my ordination date for June 8, 2019 and said, "You will now be called Elder-Elect, and we will announce it to the church on Sunday."

I said, "Wow God, that's two days before my 49th birthday. What a gift that will be."

I felt such a release because I knew that I was supposed to be ordained in my former church, but I was running from the call. Also, I was so comfortable serving on multiple ministries that I was not listening when God was calling me to the next level in the Kingdom. There were so many things God needed me to accomplish, and it couldn't be done at the level I was operating in at the present time. There was another level of anointing I needed for the next level, and I had to be ordained as an Elder to operate in it.

We had six months to prepare for my ordination. I felt so overwhelmed and excited at the same time. I felt like I was in a spiritual fight, but in reality, I was in a fight with myself. I was telling myself that I didn't feel qualified, and I didn't want to disappoint God.

I shared with Bishop how I was feeling, and Bishop said, "You should have been ordained a long time ago. I don't know why you weren't, but you've been working in the title for years. Now it's going to be official. You walk in the title before you get the title."

I don't know if Bishop realized he set me free with that word. After our conversation, I was in agreement with what God was doing in my life. As I prepared myself spiritually, mentally, and physically, I continued to press into God. I kept hearing this scripture in my spirit. *"For I know the plans I have for you, declares the Lord, plans to prosper you and not to harm you, plans to give you hope and a future."* (Jeremiah 29:11)

June 8th was approaching fast, and I still hadn't ordered my robe, stole, or cassock. I had so much to do and so little time to do it. Bishop and Pastor Ieisha were such a big help to me. I know I could not have done any of it on my own. Bishop and Pastor Ieisha put the program together and made sure everything went according to the will of God. I will be eternally grateful to them both.

The power of partnerships is so important when it comes to your purpose and destiny. When

God starts to put people in your life, make sure you don't remove the wrong ones and keep those who are not ordained to go with you to the next level. June 8, 2019 arrived, and I was so nervous but excited too. Sly was already up and moving around. He brought me my breakfast, sat on the bed and said, "Don't be nervous. It's your day, and it's a long time coming."

I finished my breakfast, and Sly grabbed my hands and started praying for me. I love that man! We arrived at the church, and I was sitting in my car watching my church family, my family, and my friends arrive. I felt so blessed to have so many people in my life that love me so much and didn't mind taking time out of their busy schedule to help make my day special. Every pastor that was a part of my ordination is so dear to me, and I love them for accepting my invitation to speak at the consecration. I will always be so very grateful and thankful to them.

It's important to know who's in your corner. As I was being robed in my vestments by Pastor Ieisha and my mother, I felt the presence of God from them both. It was such a beautiful feeling to have my mother, who introduced me to Christ, who taught me how to be a woman of integrity,

87

an honest woman, and a strong woman, be a part of my consecration ceremony. And Pastor Ieisha, who walked with me through this 15-year journey. She taught me things through her mistakes and from her successes. She wouldn't let me give up or give in when it got rough. She taught me to persevere through it all and stay in God's face.

Bishop placed his hands on me, prayed for me, and asked all the pastors to join him as he prayed. I was robed in my vestments, turned to face the congregation, and introduced to everyone as Elder Tisha Jones. What an amazing day. I will never forget how God Purposely Positioned me to walk in the shoes that only fit me.

CHAPTER 8

Conquering COVID-19: It Changes You Forever!

The Corona Virus was affecting everything and so many people around us. The virus was beginning to take a toll on many lives in every way. I knew it was serious when I received an automated phone call from my son's school stating that the school would be closing due to the Corona Virus.

My son's school closed on March 13, 2020, and I started working from home on March 16, 2020. We have been in the house since then and as I write this book, it is the middle of May. My husband is considered an essential worker because he works at a hospital, so he still had to go to work. He didn't want me to go out unless I had to, and since he was going out every day to work, he decided he would do all the shopping for the house to prevent me from going to any stores.

I would write our grocery list for Sly, and he would go food shopping before he went to work. This was an adjustment for him, because he never had to do the grocery shopping without me. He would drive me to the store and either wait in the car, or he would come in the store and keep me company. When he goes shopping now, he calls me from every aisle and makes me feel as though I am there with him, literally. We changed our daily routines to fit into our "new normal."

After about two weeks of being my son's new teacher, I was ready to quit this free job. I texted my son's teachers and praised them for what they do on a daily basis. Teachers are the real heroes too. They deserve much more than they are receiving for a salary and from the parents. This is why I give my son's teachers gifts on the holidays and recognize them on Teacher's Day. So, parents, the next time you want to believe your child and not the teacher, DON'T.

Thursday, April 2, 2020, was like any other night. It was 11:50 p.m., and I was finishing up my homework when I heard my husband coming up the steps to my study. He's usually walking up the steps about 11:30 p.m., but since we are in a horrific time because of the Corona Virus, he has a "new routine." He comes straight in from the hospital, goes to the basement, puts his clothes in the washer, and takes a shower before he enters the house. COVID-19 has changed everyone's routine, but we do what we have to do to stay safe.

I greeted my husband and asked him, how was work. He said it was good, and we began to have a conversation about his day. While we were talking, I interrupted my husband and told him that I was still having these pains in my joints and it was getting worse. He asked me what the pain felt like.

I told him, "It feels like a toothache. I have never experienced this kind of pain before."

We prayed, went to bed, and started watching T.V. I remember telling my husband, "I am really cold. Can you please turn up the heat?"

Sly got up, went downstairs, turned the heat up, and made me some hot tea. The tea didn't help much. I was shivering and cold, shaking uncontrollably.

Sly touched my forehead and said, "You have a fever."

I replied, "But I'm so cold." I got up and put on some sweatpants, a sweater, and two pairs of socks. Now my teeth were chattering. I was so cold.

Sly got up and put my housecoat and two blankets on top of me, but it didn't help, so he went to the bathroom and got two towels and wrapped them around my feet.

I woke up the next morning with my bones hurting and I just felt like I had the flu or pneumonia, I felt really bad. I didn't have an appetite. I just wanted to sleep.

Sly made me breakfast and some hot tea, but I couldn't eat anything because I had such a headache. He begged me to at least eat the toast. I sat up and opened my mouth to eat the toast, but I had such a pain in my jaws when I tried to chew, so I just drank the tea.

I slept all day and night. When I woke up Saturday morning, I had no strength and could barely lift my head due to the headache. The pain was running all down my face. All I could do was hold my face and pray. When I tried to get out of the bed, I couldn't move. Sly had to help me get up just to go to the bathroom. I knew something was wrong, and I needed to call my doctor. I called the doctor, told him how I felt, and he asked me to describe everything I felt in my body. Three minutes later, my doctor told me I had the Corona Virus and to take Tylenol for the pain and go to the emergency room if I couldn't breathe.

I hung the phone up, and tears flowed down my face. I had just received the news I was dreading to hear because I knew I had COVID-19 when my jaws hurt when I tried to eat, when I felt the toothache pains in my joints, and when I lost my sense of taste and smell. This was not the flu or pneumonia. This felt like something demonic taking over my body and trying to kill me.

My husband hugged me and said, "We will get through this together. I'm here. Just rest."

I told my husband, "You cannot stay in here with me. You have to sleep in the guest bedroom for your safety. Wear a mask around me, and please keep Caleb from coming around me too."

I never felt so isolated and more alone in my life. On April 6, 2020 my husband called my job and notified my supervisor of my illness, and then he called his job and notified his supervisor too. He told his supervisor, "I will not be back to work until my wife feels better."

His supervisor understood and gave him three weeks off. Every day, Sly would make me hot tea all day to help prevent the buildup of mucus in my lungs, he would do breathing exercises with me, and he would do chest percussions to loosen the thick, sticky, mucus from the sides of my lungs. (This helps the secretion to move into the larger airway when you take deep breaths, so you are able to cough). Sly treated himself as if he was diagnosed with the virus too just in case because he was also in quarantine due to me having the virus.

I thank God for my mother. She cooked meals for my family for three weeks and was happy to do it. My mother is a precious jewel that cannot be replaced. I love her with all my heart. If your mother is still alive, you are blessed. Appreciate your mother and give her flowers on this side of the dirt.

For the first week, I couldn't eat and still had all the symptoms of pain in my joints, jaws hurting when I tried to eat, chills, fever, dry cough, no sense of taste or smell. By the second week, I was vomiting and mentally going through a dark place. I would break down and cry at night, praying and asking God to keep me, keep my mind. I would repeat to myself, "You shall live and not die," all day and recite Psalm 91.

When I went to sleep, the constant coughing and throbbing headache would wake me up. I would look outside my bedroom door and see my husband sleeping on the floor. I felt so bad for him. I'd tell him to please go and get in the bed, but he would say, "I'm okay. I need to hear you breathing."

My dreams became darker each night. My mind was telling me I was going to die, and I started hallucinating. I would pray and ask God to heal my body, make me whole, and keep my mind stayed on Him. I would stay up all night to keep myself from dreaming and going into a dark place. Sunday, April the 19th was really bad. I was talking out of my head. I was talking to my husband and literally saw myself outside my body. I heard myself ask my husband, "Who are you?" and I began to say, "Hi," over and over again as if I didn't know him or where I was.

I started praying until I felt my mind come back to me, I laid in the bed and began to cry and thank God for His mercy and His grace on my life.

On Monday, April the 20th I woke up and was complaining that my ribs were hurting. It felt like I was being punched in the ribs every time I coughed. After an hour, I had trouble breathing.

I couldn't catch my breath, and I started hyper-ventilating. I was scared and knew this was not a good sign. I started to think about all the people who went into the hospital, never went home, and died. All I could think about was my 14-year-old son and how he just lost his father 18 months ago. I didn't want to leave him. I begged God to keep me and not let my son lose another parent. I had to pray against the spirit of fear that was trying to overtake me. *"For God has not given us a spirit of fear, but of power and of love and of a sound mind" (2Timothy 1:7).*

My husband begged me to go to the hospital, but I kept saying, "No, I don't want to go. Please don't make me go."

I felt like a child crying to her parent. Sly said, "Babe, please! You have to, because I can't sit here and let you die." He began to cry.

That's when I said yes, because I had never seen my husband cry. I was so weak. Sly had to bathe me and put my clothes on. We arrived at the hospital. I gave Sly my purse, but I kept my cell phone so I could call him. The nurse took my temperature, took all my information, told my husband he had to wait outside, and they took me away. I was put in a room by myself. It was cold, and I felt so alone, so I began to sing, "Lord be a fence all around me."

Those were the only words I could remember from the song. I prayed and asked God to allow me to go home and be with my family. I called Sly while I was waiting for the nurse to return. He told me he was in the car and would not leave me. He said he would be down the street next to the park because he was parked next to the trailer where they kept all the dead bodies, and he didn't want to see that. I called my son, and I told him I love him. I said, "I promise I'm coming home, so don't worry. Mommy is coming home."

He said, "Okay. I love you too."

The nurse came in to check my oxygen level, take an x-ray of my lungs, and give me the COVID-19 test. The room was so cold. As I looked around the room, I began to sing until I fell asleep. Thirty minutes later, the nurse returned. She said, "You have pneumonia in your lungs, but your oxygen level is good, so you do not have to stay in the hospital."

I was praising God like a crazy person. I called Sly and told him I was being released in the next twenty minutes. I said, "Please come and get me."

When we arrived home, Sly helped me out of the car and up the stairs. He took my clothes off and helped me into bed. I heard Sly on the phone talking to my doctor. He told the doctor, "You have to prescribe my wife something for her lungs before they get worse."

My doctor asked for the number to our pharmacy, and Sly picked my prescription up 30 minutes later. The doctor told Sly that the next two weeks are critical especially because I am a diabetic, and he needed to make sure I walked around upstairs, did my breathing exercises, and drank plenty of hot liquids. Two days later, the nurse called and told me my test came back positive.

For the next two weeks, I did everything I was told, and I began to feel better at the end of the two weeks. I was able to sit up in a chair for hours at a time, walk to the bathroom without help, my appetite was coming back, and my breathing was getting better. As I write this, I'm still a little weak, my taste buds are not completely back, and I still have a cough with little back and chest pains. I'm not 100 percent, but I can lift my head, get on my knees, and praise God for keeping me. I am so grateful that God spared my life. He is a promise keeper.

May 4, 2020 was the first day I was able to get on my knees and pray. I had so much to talk to God about. I cried out to God with tears of gratitude. I humbled myself before Him and thanked God for everything He has done and continues to do. I'm still weak, but I thank God for strengthening me every day. COVID-19 has changed me and my family forever. I promised God that He would always come before anyone or anything. Self-care will be my second priority, enjoying life abundantly, taking weekend trips with my family, not worrying about things I can't change, and loving people on purpose. Life is not promised to anyone. Enjoy it now.

I thank God for His mercy and His grace, my husband, for truly showing me what his wedding vows mean to him, my son for being strong, my mom for taking care of my family when I couldn't, all the pastors who reached out to me and prayed for me, the intercessors who prayed day and night, and my family and friends. I love you all!

CHAPTER 9

Matters Of The Heart

Things I wish I could have told myself as a young girl...and now I say to you:
You are loved. You are special. You are beautiful. Their words are not meant to kill you. The trials will strengthen you, build character in you, and you will do great things for the Kingdom. Remember, don't let the words of others burn out your light within.

Growing up was emotionally difficult for me because I felt like I was different, and I never felt I belonged. Even though I have a twin sister and we grew up very close to one another, I always felt I had to do more to fit in.

If I only knew who I was then, I would have made so many different choices. I know now why I had to go through the things I went through. Life has a way of preparing you and teaching you for trials and disappointments you will face, but if you choose not to die, you will come out on top.

-Tisha Jones

Purposely Positioned

Poetic Expressions

Loving Me

The seeds that were planted in me confused me about who you created me to be. I was born to worship you, but I hid myself in guilt and shame because I felt unlovable. When I confessed my sins and secrets to you, you freed me; and now the love I feel from your divine presence has given me the courage and responsibility to speak into other women who suffer in the same secrets you freed me from.

-Tisha Jones

A Beautiful Flower

You spoke to me in visions
You spoke to me in dreams
To prepare me for this life that can be so mean
The words spoken over me
The seeds planted in me
Little by little devalued me
But as your Word watered my seeds
I grew up with more flowers than weeds
Look at my flowers as they blossom and bloom
Soon my roots will need more room
Because of the strength from your Word
This little girl grew up demanding to be heard

-Tisha Jones

My Voice

Now I have a voice that's loud and clear
Watch out devil I no longer walk in fear
I talk to other women
while fighting back the tears
Knowing I have so much more
hurt and pain to hear
I wish I could tell them,
soon all the scars will be wiped clear
Let go, let go of the shame and guilt
my sweet little dear
We have a heavenly Father
who loves us and holds us near
The things you faced in life
were never meant for you to bear

-Tisha Jones

Butterfly

The caterpillar has now become a butterfly
I'm free, I'm free no longer held, I can fly
Oh, can you see how the world
looks through my eyes
I see shapes and colors because I can fly so high
No more hurt, no more pain I no longer cry
What can hold me back now
from flying in the sky
No longer hiding or believing the devil's lies
Don't you know now,
I'm a child of the Most High

-Tisha Jones

ABOUT THE AUTHOR

Pastor **Tisha Jones** is an anointed, vivacious and powerful woman of God, called to be a servant of the Lord. The ministry that God has placed inside of her is powerful, positive, bold, effective, and vital to the body of Christ. The capacity in which He uses her in the Servant's Ministry can be seen through the glory and the presence of the Almighty. God uses her ministry to transform lives and stimulate effective change in the body of Christ.

Pastor Jones surrendered her will to the will of God in 2000. She has grown tremendously over the years and has dedicated her life to serving in many offices in ministry. She serves as Administrative Pastor at Bethel Total Man Ministries, Hackensack, NJ under the leadership of Bishop T. Raynard Randall. She is also the Associate Pastor of a new church plant, BOLD Ministries, in Irvington, New Jersey under the leadership of Bishop Randall.

Pastor Tisha Jones has served as a Minister, Adjutant, Pastoral Care Ministry, Paraments Ministry, and Intercessor. She has also trained other leaders how to serve in the capacity of an Adjutant or Armor Bearers with a spirit of excellence. **Pastor Jones** has been married since 2012 to her King, Sylvester Jones and has one son, Master Caleb Isaiah Woodley. She loves spending quality time with family and friends, she's an avid reader and a frequent mover goer. She is currently employed with the State of New Jersey as a Child Support Specialist. She graduated from the New York School of the Bible in Manhattan, NY in 2016. She also attended Lancaster Bible College in Lancaster, PA where she received a bachelor's degree in Biblical Studies.

Pastor Jones' passion for reading has birthed out the ministry, "Daughters of Deborah" book club. Over the span of 10 years, the book club has grown to over 25 women. The purpose of Daughters of Deborah book club is to help women understand their self-worth, their purpose, their destiny and calling so they can operate in the spirit of excellence to edify the body of Christ while striving to walk in the will and the ways of God. She is now a published author with her first book release titled, "**Purposely Positioned.**"

Pastor Jones has a God-ordained ministry for women. Her passion is to help women prosper in all facets of their lives. She encourages women to transform their lives by seeking God through His Word, workshops, retreats, conferences and practicing self-care. She encourages, inspires, and uplifts individuals, through creative coaching and mentoring. Her love for people radiates through her dedication and spirit of excellence in ministry.

ORDER INFORMATION

You can order additional copies of Purposely
Positioned by emailing the author directly using
the email address below.

Pastor Tisha Jones

Email Address:

purposelypositioned50@gmail.com

Books are available at Amazon.com, BN.com
Kindle and Your Local Bookstores (By Request)

Please leave a review for this book on Amazon and let other readers know how much you enjoyed reading it.

Thank you!

Made in the USA
Middletown, DE
25 August 2023